Robins

Wil Mara

New York

Published in 2015 by Cavendish Square Publishing, LLC
243 5th Avenue, Suite 136, New York, NY 10016

First Edition

Website: cavendishsq.com

This publication represents the opinions and views of the author based on his or her personal experience, knowledge, and research. The information in this book serves as a general guide only. The author and publisher have used their best efforts in preparing this book and disclaim liability rising directly or indirectly from the use and application of this book.

CPSIA Compliance Information: Batch #WS14CSQ

All websites were available and accurate when this book was sent to press.

Library of Congress Cataloging-in-Publication Data

Mara, Wil.
Robins / Wil Mara.
pages cm. — (Backyard safari)
Includes index.
ISBN 978-1-62712-825-4 (hardcover) ISBN 978-1-62712-826-1 (paperback) ISBN 978-1-62712-827-8 (ebook)
1. American robin—Juvenile literature. I. Title.

QL696.P288M356 2014
598.8'42--dc23

2013047683

Editorial Director: Dean Miller
Editor: Andrew Coddington
Copy Editor: Cynthia Roby
Art Director: Jeffrey Talbot
Designer: Joseph Macri
Photo Researcher: J8 Media
Production Manager: Jennifer Ryder-Talbot
Production Editor: David McNamara

The photographs in this book are used by permission and through the courtesy of: Cover photo by David & Micha Sheldon/F1online/Getty Images; Mother Daughter Press/Photographer's Choice/Getty Images, 4; age fotostock/SuperStock, 6; Animals Animals/SuperStock, 9; Photographer who enjoys experimenting with various styles/Flickr Open/Getty Images 10; Mike Harrington/Taxi/Getty Images, 11; © iStockphoto.com/Frank Leung, 13; Radius/SuperStock, 17; © Anderson, Vickie/Animals Animals, 19; © Wild & Natural/Animals Animals, 20; Michael S. Quinton/National Geographic/Getty Images, 22; Panoramic Images/Panoramic Images/Getty Images, 22; Darlyne A. Murawski/National Geographic/Getty Images, 22; Tom Vezo/Minden Pictures/Getty Images, 22; © jack thomas/Alamy, 23; Nordic Photos/SuperStock, 26; © Kuttig - People/Alamy, 28.

Printed in the United States of America

Contents

Introduction 4

ONE A Robin's Life 5

TWO You Are the Explorer 11

THREE A Guide to Robins 19

FOUR Try This! Projects You Can Do 23

Glossary 29

Find Out More 30

Index 31

Introduction

Have you ever watched a squirrel chasing another squirrel around a tree, or a group of deer leaping gracefully through a stretch of winter woods? If you have, then you know how wonderful it is to discover nature for yourself. Each book in the Backyard Safari series takes you step-by-step on an easy outdoor adventure, then helps you identify the animals you've found. You'll also learn ways to attract, observe, and protect these valuable creatures. As you read, be on the lookout for the Safari Tips and Trek Talk facts sprinkled throughout the book. Ready? The fun starts just steps from your back door!

ONE
A Robin's Life

The American Robin, also known simply as the robin, is a relatively small bird. It measures only about 10 inches (25 centimeters) in length and usually weighs close to 3 ounces (85 grams). The robin's **wingspan**— meaning when its wings are fully opened and spread out—measures around 14 inches (36 cm).

The robin's head is round-shaped and varies in color from dark to medium gray, with a black eye that is often ringed in white. Its bill is one of several shades of yellow with a bit of dark coloration on the tip. Sometimes it has a distinct orange tint. But it can, on occasion, look so pale that it appears white. There will be patches of white on its throat, belly, and under the tail feathers, which are often streaked with narrow dark lines. The robin's back is usually some shade of brown or gray.

The robin's most significant feature is the reddish-orange color of its chest feathers, which is why it is also called "robin redbreast." In males, this coloration can be very vivid, whereas the overall color tones of the females are usually a bit duller. Newborn robins may have only a faint reddish-orange coloration on their chest, which will instead have a white base with dark spotting.

Where They Live

The robin is one of the most common birds in North America. It is found as far north as Alaska and Canada, as far south as Central Mexico, and along both the eastern and western coasts. It is important to note that the robin is commonly a migrating bird, which means it changes its home **range** depending on the season. For example, a robin living in the American northeast in the spring and summer may **migrate** to the southwest during the colder months. Then again, those who live in the more moderate climates of North America—states where it never gets overly cold or warm—will likely stay in one general area year round.

Robins are among the most common birds in all of North America and can be found in a variety of habitats.

Trek Talk

Robins are among the most abundant birds in all of North America. It is believed that there are more than 300 million living robins at any one time in the wild! And those 300 million cover a home range of about six million square miles (15.5 million square kilometers)! Happily, this means the American Robin is not considered to be a threatened or an endangered **species**. Nevertheless, it is still protected by federal law through what is called the Migratory Bird Act. This law forbids people from hunting, killing, capturing, or selling robins (and other species, too). This means there are plenty of robins for you to find on your safari.

Migrating robins will begin leaving their warm-weather homes in late summer or early fall, then return in late winter. Florida and the Gulf Coast states are favorite wintering areas. Parts of Mexico as well as the southern areas of the Pacific coast are also preferred. Robins have also been spotted as far south as Jamaica, Puerto Rico, and the island of Hispaniola (where both the Dominican Republic and Haiti are located), and as far north as Greenland, which reaches into the Arctic Ocean and nearly to the North Pole!

The robin is an interesting bird in terms of **habitat**. It can thrive in a surprising variety of **environments**, although it seems most comfortable in quiet forests and around farmlands. Beyond that, they have been known to build nests on the ledges of buildings, on telephone poles, and on the fixtures (such as below the edge of a roof or behind a trellis) of homes. As long as they have suitable cover allowing them to live in safety, robins will find a place to settle down. They also prefer to nest off the ground and thus spend much of their time in trees.

What They Do

Robins are **diurnal** creatures—that is, they carry out most of their activities during daylight hours (as opposed to nighttime, or **nocturnal** animals). It is not unusual to see them moving about individually during the day, but at sunset they often gather in huge numbers.

The robin is a very musical bird. It sings frequently throughout the day during the warmer months. Its "song" is usually made up of a few notes at a time, often strung together as if the bird is trying to create a melody. The robin's tunes have been described as cheerful and uplifting. They are very often the first birds to be heard singing at sunrise.

The robin spends a great deal of its waking hours searching for food. The majority of its diet consists of fruits, particularly berries. The remainder is made up of whatever small **invertebrates** the robin can catch, including bugs of all kinds and, of course, earthworms. The image of a robin with one end of an earthworm in its beak and tugging like mad to yank the rest of it from the ground is a familiar one. A robin can hunt for invertebrates by both scent and sound, but it primarily uses its sight to find such **prey**.

Robins are active during the day and spend much of their time foraging for food. Their favorite items are berries and small invertebrates.

The Cycle of Life

Robins begin their breeding cycle shortly after returning from their wintering homes. This is usually during the late winter or early spring. Female robins are responsible for building the nest. They do this by gathering twigs and small branches, tough grasses, feathers (both their own and those of other birds), and even some man-made materials, such as bits of paper or cardboard. Nests can take about five or six days to finish. They are built high off the ground and are usually tucked protectively behind dense leaf clusters or layers of overgrowth.

Robins are not afraid to build nests in areas where a lot of people move about. Both the male and female will defend their nests if they feel threatened. They will make shrill alarm calls and then swoop down to attack any potential **predators**.

The average number of eggs a robin will lay at one time is four, although only about one in every four newborns will survive into adulthood. These eggs can be distinguished by their beautiful greenish-blue color. The eggs hatch after about two weeks. At that time, all day long, both parents will hunt for insects to feed the newborns, which are called **hatchlings**. After another two weeks the hatchlings, then called **fledglings**, are fully feathered and leave their parents' nest. The average lifespan for a robin in the wild is roughly two years.

Robins hatch about two weeks after their eggs are laid, and they will leave their parents' nest roughly two weeks after that.

TWO
You Are the Explorer

Bird watching is one of the most relaxing, pleasant, and rewarding outdoor activities imaginable. There are millions of people around the world, of all ages, who enjoy the birding pastime. Robins make particularly good study subjects because they are so abundant throughout North America and are relatively comfortable around humans. Once you understand the importance of giving them their space without disturbing them, you will begin to see for yourself the fascinating lives they lead.

What Do I Wear?

* Old clothes that can get dirty
* Clothes that are loose-fitting and comfortable
* A jacket, gloves, hat, and other warm clothing if you are going out during cold weather
* Clothes that are not too bright or vivid in color. Remember—you don't want to disturb, distract, or frighten the robins.
* Any type of shoes will do, but those with soft soles will be the quietest. The less noise you make the better. Also, if you have to do a lot of walking, you'll want to be comfortable. In the winter, you might need boots.
* Bug spray, particularly if you're going into forested areas near waterways

What Do I Take?

* Binoculars. Since you really shouldn't try to get too close to a live robin, a good pair of binoculars will be the most important piece of equipment you can bring along on your safari.
* Notebook

* Pen or pencil
* Folding chair or blanket
* Digital camera, particularly one that can retain good focus while zooming
* A cell phone
* A snack for yourself

Where Do I Go?

You're very lucky in that robins are adaptable to a wide variety of habitats. From the country to the city and everywhere in between, there's a fairly good chance you'll be able to find a few robins nesting and flying around close to your home. Remember that robins spend the majority of their time off the ground. They usually come down only to munch on insects or snatch up fruits and berries that have fallen from trees or vines. Occasionally they will also touch down to fight off predators or other robins that are invading their territory (robins can be quite **territorial** at times). But again, most of the robins you spot will likely be flying or perched somewhere.

* Open woodlands. Robins seem to prefer forested areas that aren't too crowded with trees.

They don't require the same degree of privacy and cover as some other birds, except when caring for their young (in which case their nests can be almost impossible to find). A good spot to check out is a short cluster of trees in an otherwise developed neighborhood—that is a row of about ten or twenty trees on a suburban block.

* Farmlands. A smart robin knows that it can always find a meal on a busy farm. Smart safari enthusiasts know that they will be able to find a few robins within that same area. A farm is one place where you will want to keep a close eye on your surroundings. There will be many crawly things about, as well as a great deal of fallen fruits and berries.

* Thick shrubs and other overgrowth. During the spring months— which is breeding season—robins will build their nests in wild places where they feel their young will be most protected. This means they will choose trees with heavy canopies, thick shrubs, and any other area that has deep overgrowth. Even after the fledglings have started their own lives, adult robins will sometimes linger in the nests for a little while. It's very important to note, however, that robins, which are usually fairly good- natured, will be more nervous and temperamental during this

time. If you do see a robin flying to and from its nest, you are still free to observe it—but don't get too close. Remember—they can become aggressive and even violent if they feel threatened.

✳ High spots in busy towns and cities. You might not believe how common robins are in more densely populated areas. If you live in such a place, there's a good chance of spotting a robin simply by scanning the ledges of buildings, along light fixtures, atop billboards, and on rooftops. Robins don't seem particularly disturbed by all the activity going on below them. And those that have lived in that same environment throughout several generations are probably used to it.

Safari Tip
A good place to look for a robin's nest is at the farthest edge of a tree branch. Robins will build their nests this far out because that makes it harder for mammal predators, such as squirrels and cats, to get to them.

Remember that you should always be with an adult that you trust when you go on a robin safari. It can be dangerous for you to walk around alone. Similarly, if you go on someone else's property, make sure that you have permission to do so. You can get into serious trouble for trespassing. Farms, for example, are a great place to find robins—but not if you aren't allowed to be there.

What Do I Do?

✳ Go out during the day. Remember that robins are diurnal creatures, which means you won't find them at night. The best time to locate robins is very early in the morning. That's when they are fully rested and ready for their daily activities. There will be many of them about, hunting for food and making their usual sounds. Which leads to a second tip…

✳ Listen. Robins are very musical, and this helps you tremendously. You should go online and listen to sound samples of their songs and their calls. Expert bird enthusiasts know how to identify many bird species simply by the sounds they make. This is something you can learn how to do, too. Once you've memorized that distinct robin sound, you'll be amazed how easily you locate one in the wild. Locating them by sound is also beneficial in that they are sometimes difficult to see—but their distinct melodies always give them away.

Binoculars are useful on robin safaris because they enable you to observe the birds without getting too close, which will only serve to scare them off.

❇ Don't make too much noise or movement. Robins, like most other wild animals, will quickly become nervous in the company of humans. Once you've located a robin or two (or more), plant yourself in a good observation spot and stay there. If you limit your sounds and your movements, the robins will relax and go about their business. This is exactly what you want—to watch them "do their thing."

* Be patient. You may not spot a robin within the first ten minutes of your safari. That's normal, and it's perfectly fine. Robins live in the wild all the time and are experts at sensing danger. This means they'll probably know you're there long before you know *they're* there.

* Keep your camera ready at all times. It's always rewarding to capture a few great pictures of robins in the wild, so you need to be ready for such opportunities. Don't leave your camera off thinking that you'll have plenty of time when a robin lands nearby. Also, avoid using a flash if you can help it. It could frighten the robins.

* Make notes. After you've observed a few robins, write down any information that you feel is important. What were they doing? Where were you when you saw them? What time of day was it? After you gather enough data, you'll begin to recognize patterns that'll help you with future safaris.

* When you return home, download any pictures (or videos, since most cameras take those as well) you took. Show them to your friends and family. You could also write a formal journal using both your pictures and your notes. Keep an ongoing record of your robin safaris from year to year.

THREE
A Guide to Robins

There is only one species of American Robin. And although seven subspecies exist within that species, the robins do not look that different from each other. The fact that robin subspecies can be found within the same area and within the same range (and at varying times of the year) may make them even more difficult to identify without careful observation. Here are some important points that should help you identify the species you encounter.

Referring back to the notes you made while on your safari, consider the following questions:

 ❊ Did the bird already have its distinctive, bright reddish-orange coloration on its chest? If not, it may have been a very young specimen.

 ❊ Were the chest feathers more orange or more reddish?

 ❊ Was the overall coloration of the bird fairly bright, or was it more somber, meaning almost dull? This is one way you can often tell males and females apart.

 ❊ Was there light coloration on and around the head, or was it almost entirely dark?

 ❊ Was there gray coloring on the tips of the head fathers?

 ❊ Did the bird look like an adult, yet had almost no reddish-orange coloration on the chest? Some older females in the western part of the range exhibit very little of this coloring.

Always look for the distinctive reddish-orange coloring on a robin's chest. Almost all wild specimens will have it.

By matching the colors, size, and other **characteristics** with the photos in the robin guide, you should be able to identify other species you see on safari. Here is a sample entry:

AMERICAN ROBIN
- Color(s): Black-grey wings and tail; orangish chest and belly
- Size: About 8–10 inches (20–25 cm)
- Location: Perched on the branch of a tree in my backyard
- Activity: Flapping his wings and singing

Robins are among the most common birds in North America. There are many subspecies all over the United States and Canada. Robins can thrive in many environments and climates, from temperate cities to chilly tundra to subtropical forests. This means that wherever you live, robins are likely to be living near you! Now, go to the next page and see if any of the robins in the photos match the characteristics that you noted in your answers. Remember that you should use other information, such as your location (town, state, and country).

Alaska

North Carolina

Massachusetts

Arizona

FOUR

Try This!
Projects You Can Do

You shouldn't keep a robin as a pet, and you certainly can't fly up to a robin's nest and live there! You can further your interest in robins through other hands-on ways when you're not out there on a safari, though. The following are a few easy and enjoyable projects you might want to consider.

House Building

Building a birdhouse for a robin and then placing it on your property can be a lot of fun. The most important detail to remember is that robins, unlike a lot of other bird species, will not be looking for the kind of house in which they will be completely hidden. A very simple house for a robin, therefore, only needs a base, a roof, and walls on the left and right sides. (Make sure to leave the front and back wide open so the robins can fly in and out.)

What Do I Need?

* Wood
* A hammer and nails
* Paint (optional)
* Tree or wooden pole

What Do I Do?

* After you have gathered your materials, begin constructing the birdhouse. The roof and the base do not need to be any larger than 8 inches (20 cm) square. The walls should be roughly the same in width, and with a height of no more than 10 inches (25 cm).

* You can add whatever colorful designs you wish. The robins won't mind. Painting the house brown or green will help it blend with its natural surroundings. Make sure to only use water-based paints. Birds could have a reaction to paints that are oil-based.

* Pick a quiet area in your backyard to place your birdhouse. You may either hang the birdhouse off the side of a tree or place it on top of a pole. It should be at least 7 feet (2 meters) off the ground.

You should always have an adult help you with such a project, of course, since it will probably require the use of power tools.

Feeding Time

Like all living things, robins need to eat every day. They will appreciate any help you can give them in gathering food.

What Do I Need?

* Robins will take nearly any fruit you can spare, including cherries, strawberries, bayberries, elderberries, blueberries, grapes, raisins, apples (cut up), and raspberries.

* Robins also like mealworms, which some people may find gross, but these worms are in fact fairly healthy for robins. They can be purchased at nearly any pet shop.
* A cup or bowl

What Do I Do?

* Although you're feeding birds, you don't necessarily need to put up a bird feeder. Instead, simply pile the food into your cup or bowl and set it down near the spot where the robins are living.

Robins will greatly appreciate any food item you leave out for them, and berries are always a good choice.

Robin 9-1-1

During one of your safaris you might encounter a robin that is sick or wounded. It would be moving unusually slow or lying on the ground and hardly moving at all. In such cases, you may be tempted to get close to it in an attempt to help. Don't. First, you'll probably frighten the robin so badly that it will become even more sick. And second, birds are known to carry an array of diseases that can be very harmful to humans. If you have an adult with you (which you should), ask that person to call your local animal control organization (most towns have them), zoo, or police department. If you see a robin that is suffering, be smart and let someone else take care of the situation—don't try to handle it on your own.

❋ Keep a careful watch to make sure other animals don't steal the food before the robins notice that it is there. It's also worth noting that your robins will be particularly grateful if you put out food for them during the colder months. That is the time when food in the wild is harder to find.

Chit Chat

One of the reasons robins make sounds is to communicate with each other. And while it isn't a good idea to try to physically touch a robin, you can get in contact with one in another way: by talking to it in its own language.

What Do I Need?

❋ Your hands and voice

❋ A bush or tree to hide behind

What Do I Do?

❋ First, learn as many robin sounds as possible. This can be done easily enough with the aid of the Internet, where you'll find hundreds of robin sound files.

❋ Practice imitating these sounds until you feel that you've got them down pat. They don't have to be perfect, but try to get as close as possible. When you spot a robin on one of your next safaris, listen first to the sounds it's making, then try to make the same sound on your own. The real excitement will come when you draw the bird's attention to you— and even better, when you get it to "call back."

If you can learn how to imitate robin sounds, you will greatly increase your chances of drawing their interest.

Glossary

characteristic a specific trait or quality that an animal has, such as tan fur or brown eyes

diurnal active during the day

environment the general type of place where an animal lives, such as a forest, swamp, or desert

habitat the exact type of place in which an animal lives, such as a burrow, cave, or shoreline

invertebrate an animal that does not have a backbone

migrate to move from one place to another

nocturnal active during the night

predator an animal that hunts other animals for food

prey any animal that is hunted by another for food

range the general area in which an animal lives

species one particular type of animal

territorial a word that describes an animal that is protective of the area in which it lives

wingspan the tip-to-tip length of a bird's wings when fully extended

Find Out More

Books

Cate, Annette LeBlanc. *Look Up! Bird-watching in Your Own Backyard.* Somerville, MA: Candlewick Press, 2013.

Porter, Adele. *Wild About Northeastern Birds: A Youth's Guide.* Cambridge, MN: Adventure Publications, 2010.

Truit, Trudi Strain. *Birds.* New York, NY: Cavendish Square, 2011.

Websites

American Robin Facts for Kids / Nature Mapping Program
www.naturemappingfoundation.org/natmap/facts/american_robin_k6.html
Lots of basic facts, some very good photos of robins, plus links to other useful sites.

The American Robin / National Geographic
animals.nationalgeographic.com/animals/birding/american-robin
Tons of information about the American robin, along with some beautiful illustrations, a range map, and some audio files.

American Robin / Cornell Lab of Ornithology
www.allaboutbirds.org/guide/american_robin/sounds
A terrific selection of easy-to-play robin sound files that includes songs and calls from different times of the day or night.

Index

Page numbers in **boldface** are illustrations.

characteristic, 21

diurnal, 8, 16

environment, 8, 15, 21

fledgling, 10, 14
food preferences, 8-9, 25-26

habitat, **6**, 8, 13
hatchling, 10

invertebrate, 8, 9, **9**

mating, 9-10
migrate, 6

nocturnal, 8

physical characteristics, 5, 19, 20-21
predator, 10, 13, 15
prey, 9

range, 6, 7, 19, 20
American Robin, 5, 7, 19, 21
    Alaska robin, **22**
    Arizona robin, **22**
    Massachusetts robin, **22**
    North Carolina robin, **22**

species, 7, 16, 19, 21, 24

territorial, 13

wingspan, 5

About the Author

WIL MARA is the award-winning author of more than 140 books. He began his writing career with several titles about herpetology—the study of reptiles and amphibians. Since then he has branched out into other subject areas and continues to write educational books for children. To find out more about Mara's work, you can visit his website at www.wilmara.com.